Quiet Time
Setting our Heart on God

This book on **Quiet Time** is part of the Ezra 7:10 ™ series of publications. It is also part of a larger three-book discipleship program called the *Ezra 7:10 Plan*. Specifically **Quiet Time** is a *Disciple Skill* included as part of Book 1 - ***First Love:*** *A Heart to Understand*. For more information about this plan please go to the program web site at http://www.ezra710plan.org

Quiet Time
Setting our Heart on God

Geoseff Obadiah Doulos

Cover Graphic: Heart_sweetheartValentine –by Jouni Paavilainen:
www.ChristianPhotos.Net

Editor-in-Chief: Judy Kissinger

Quiet Time: *Setting our Heart on God*

Copyright © 2010 by Geoseff Doulos
Front Royal, VA 22630

Ezra 710 publications
ISBN – 13: 978-0-61542-850-5
ISBN – 10: 0-61542-850-9

To the Glory of God

Contents

Quiet Time
Setting our Heart on God

The Ezra 7$\frac{10}{}$ Plan *1st Love*

Quiet Time
Setting our Heart on God

The single most important thing that we will ever do in our life will be to spend time with the Lord. The term "Quiet Time" has been coined in relatively recent Christian circles to describe this time alone with the Lord. If we make it the number-one priority of our life each day, our life will be blessed, we will be a blessing, and we will experience a relationship with God as never before. We will also experience a peace, a purpose, and a plan for our life that will instill in us a quiet yet bold confidence to face whatever may lie ahead.

The next five sections will prepare us to begin (or re-energize) our lifelong relationship with the Lord. First we look at why this time is so important and so exciting. *Our Father* discusses not just why we need to do this, but also the fact that the Lord Himself has done everything He can to make having a close relationship with Him possible. *Our Failures* candidly talks about some common pitfalls and distractions that prevent us from a quality relationship with God. Next, *Our Fruit* is basically a mini Bible study of the *Parable of the Sower*. In this section we will learn about the fruits of spending time with the Lord. *Our Fruit* is both inspiring and sobering. In the following section, *Our Focus,* we relay some very tangible ways to get the most out of our time with the Lord of Glory. Finally in the last section, *Our Field,* we teach how to pass this knowledge onto others who may be in our field of view and in our sphere of influence. We become equipped to teach others in our own words how to experience Quiet Time.

As in all Ezra 7:10 publications, we will be informed, we will be given ways to practice this new knowledge and we will be equipped to teach others what we have just learned.

Our Father

Experiencing God

Do we realize that God is our Father in the truest sense of the word? He not only created us physically, but He also provided the way by which we can be born again spiritually, and abide with Him for all eternity. From day one, He has desired the best for us. Even though we stray from Him, He always holds out His hand to guide us back. One of the amazing things to remember about our Father is that *He never gives up on people.*

His first goal after He brought us into this world was to provide a means whereby we can fellowship with Him. Even though we stubbornly went our own way apart from Him, He kept nudging us to realize the error of our ways so we could yield ourselves completely to His perfect plan for us. As in the *Parable of the Lost Sheep*, He went out to search for one little lost lamb to bring him to a place where life could be lived to the fullest. That clearly shows how much *He cares about us.* Now this is the kind of person we want to get to know.

14

By now, perhaps we are somewhat familiar with the doctrine of sin and salvation, but let us go over this again, to understand fully and appreciate how great is our God. Of course everyone in the world has been originally separated from our true Father because of sin and the desire to do things his own way. We might not have thought of ourselves as particularly evil or sinful, but in God's eyes whatever does not proceed from the truth or faith in His word is sinful. We do not have to think of sin in terms of evil, but in terms of incompatibility with God. God cannot be in the presence of sin; therefore anything sinful must be separated from Him. God's way of providing sinful man a way to approach a holy God is through atonement. He recognized that we were incapable of being sinless, but if our sin could be atoned for we would have the ability to approach Him. *It is clear that the Lord cherishes communing with us and blessing us.*

One place this atonement or salvation message is contained is in Isaiah chapter 53.

Isaiah 53:6 *All of us like sheep have gone astray, Each of us has turned to his own way; But the*

LORD has caused the iniquity of us all To fall on Him.

So we see this verse describes the state that we were in before we received an actual pardon for our sins. The verse does not describe our condition as evil. It uses the terms *gone astray* and *turned to his own way.* Nevertheless this condition is evil and idolatrous to the Lord. Why dwell so long on this particular discussion?

First of all, as we have said before, it shows us the great lengths that God has taken for our benefit (i.e., His plan for our redemption from day one, culminating in the death of His own Son Jesus Christ).

Second, it shows that since He has taken such care to save us from the penalty of our sins, He must want to show the same care in guiding and blessing us. How can anything compare to spending time with a person such as this?

Finally, *since God has gone to great lengths for us, we should go to great lengths with Him.*

Let us now go back to the beginning of our spiritual journey. To some that is not too long ago and for some it is ancient history. By going back to our spiritual start we can check to see if our spiritual priorities are still where they should be or if we need to make any changes.

When we became a follower of Christ through our profession of faith, we probably were baptized, and joined a fellowship of believers, doing Bible study, etc. We may have experienced quite a few character changes, and have made some lifestyle changes as well. Rebirth leads to re-growth, and all is well and exciting. But amidst these Christian activities we must remember that at the heart of everything is God. Our new life is not just a life of new activities and new relationships. At the core of it all we need to let it sink in that God truly is our Father, and we are his children. *Do we need to break away from the hustle and bustle and rejuvenate our relationship with our heavenly Father?*

Depending on what age we were when we first became believers, this concept (God as our Father) may be easy or it may be difficult to grasp. Also, our family background — such as whether we had a good father or a father who abandoned us — may make a difference in how we initially handle our new relationship with our Father God. Make no mistake about this point though, "God is good all the time and all the time, God is good." We can also exchange "good" with "love." If we grasp this one single principle, we will be well on our way to developing a close personal relationship with our Father. *Do we need to remind ourselves again of the deep love God has for us?*

Changing leadership or instructors can be difficult (for example at work or school). As a new Christian we have the ultimate change of leadership. We ourselves are no longer in charge; someone even better, the Lord, is now in charge. We are no longer following our old ways but are seeking to follow God's ways. The great thing about being a child of God though, is just that — *we have God as our Father! Do we need to give God back the reins of leadership we may have subtly taken back?*

When we meet with the Lord each day we are not just meeting with a friend, or a general, or a task master, or a physician, or a judge, or a farmer, or a master designer, or a physical therapist, or a counselor (the list is endless); in fact, we are meeting with all of these in one Person, who also happens to be our Father. This should inspire reverence, joy and yes, a little fear (in a good way). *Do we need to remind ourselves that God is our source of total supply?*

It is hoped this review was helpful and we can implement any needed changes. Now it is time to end with an exhortation to keep running the race well with our relationship with God as the number one priority in our lives.

Quiet Time helps ensure that we will not stray too far from God and His ways. The apostle Paul, in the Book of 2 Timothy chapter two, likens hardships we will face to different occupations such as a soldier, a farmer and an athlete. Yet amidst these adversities of life we must always remember that God is guiding us as a Father who is raising his children (our age does not matter). Ultimately the goal is to know God Himself fully and to be able to recognize God's fingerprints in our lives and the lives we touch. We will be able to discern God's will, God's voice and God's unmistakable handiwork. *We will view with awe not just his handiwork in creation, but in re-creation — that would be us!*

It is not the intent of this exhortation on Quiet Time to fill the pages with Bible verses so that it becomes a Bible study in itself. We can do that on our own time (which would be an excellent investment of time). Suffice to say, there are many verses that talk about the need for us to spend time with the Lord every single day. This will help us learn His ways and to walk in them and to have a close personal relationship with God.

From the beginning of time until the present, our knowledge of God has been given to us in different ways. But even those folks who lived before Moses and the written Law had learned plenty from the Lord through a variety of sources. We can be sure that Enoch, Noah, Job and of course David, had Quiet Times with the Lord. Even a cursory reading of Job makes it clear that he knew the Lord well, not perfectly of course, but very well. Where did his

knowledge of God come from? Read the Book
of Job for the answer. The Bible as we know it
was not in existence way back then, but the
need to spend time with the Lord and learn
about his ways was obviously as important then
as it is now. David is one of the best examples.
He had a very close and insightful relationship
with the Lord, even though he had access to
just the first five books of the Bible (The
Pentateuch). If we read the Psalms of David we
can get a glimpse of where he discovered the
ways and teachings of God. From the Psalms it
is very clear that he meditated on the
Scriptures that were available to him, but he
also discovered other aspects about God
through other experiences. Those same
experiences are available to us today. Read the
Psalms to discover these wonderful (and
sometimes not so wonderful) experiences that
God uses to manifest Himself to us.

So often new Christians become lax in their
time and allow the things of the world to creep
in, and they lose their ability to distinguish
what is of the Lord and what is not. Too often
they cannot see or hear the Lord any more.
This may be especially true as believers get

older. The Old Testament has numerous examples of this (e.g., Solomon, Lot, Jereboam, etc.).

It is difficult to start out well and to finish well. But the Bible was written to give us a roadmap for spiritual success. That is why our Quiet Time is the single most important thing we can do. Every spiritual decline in the Bible is initially due to spending less and less time with God. Conversely, every spiritual revival begins with a renewal to spend time with God on a daily basis to learn His Word and His ways.

If we can commit ourselves to spending some time with our Father God every single day of our lives without fail, we will have prepared ourselves adequately for the long haul, for finishing well. *To cross the finish line with joy, looking forward to spending the rest of eternity with the Lord, our true Father forever, to not fear death, will be a great feeling.* How sad for some, who perhaps in their last few days on earth, spend it in *sackcloth and ashes* repenting of their past complacencies and their worldly entanglements. While *better late than never* is certainly true with respect to our salvation and our service to the Lord, yet why not take a spiritual performance review now and every year to make sure we are on the right track? Let us leave this world with no regrets or as few regrets as possible.

Why talk about the end of life on earth now, when this is supposed to be an exhortation on how to run the race well? Simply put, the end goal determines our plan of action. Even if we are young, it does not hurt to attend a few funerals, or to visit a courtroom. We will realize with certainty that life on earth has a sure end, and that judgment once pronounced is final. Can we live each day as if it is our last?

Ecclesiastes 7:2-5 *It is better to go to a house of mourning Than to go to a house of feasting, Because that is the end of every man, And the living takes it to heart. Sorrow is better than laughter, For when a face is sad a heart may be happy. The mind of the wise is in the house of mourning, While the mind of fools is in the house of pleasure. It is better to listen to the rebuke of a wise man Than for one to listen to the song of fools.*

Yes, too often we can become complacent about how much time we have even though the Bible is full of exhortations to make the most of our time. How do we fall into this trap? You guessed it. Our daily time with the Lord slips and is gradually replaced by something else. Seems so simple, yet the ways of the world are subtle. We must guard our hearts and minds so we mimic the Lord's ways and not the world's ways. The side paths off the straight and narrow are many and we must wear blinders to a certain extent to make sure we do not step to the left or to the right.

Psalm 44:18 *Our heart has not turned back, And our steps have not deviated from Your way,*

To start off well in the Christian life is vital for a successful finish. We do not want to sow any tares (weeds) among the wheat so early (or at any time for that matter) in our Christian walk.

We must remember the single most important thing about being a Christian is having a deepening relationship with our Father God. Quiet Time is the key. As each year passes, we should keep asking ourselves whether or not our actions and activities are drawing us closer to God or farther away. When God seems far away guess who moved? The next section, *Our Failures*, helps us stay close to God by showing us what to avoid!

Our Failures

Extinguishing God

This section details some traps to avoid, thus making the most of our time here on earth while we are *in the world* but not *of the world*.

So if one of the keys to the Christian life is to spend quality time with the Lord, then what do we think the enemy of God (read: Satan) is going to do about this? He is going to try and sidetrack us and subtly distract us by getting us *hooked* on other activities that compete for this time that we have devoted to the Lord.

A look at two simple words, *amusement* and *entertainment*, and their word origins will help us see this plan of the enemy. All definitions in this section are from *Merriam-Webster, I. (1996, c1993)*.

The word *amusement* literally means *to not think*. The word *muse* means *to think* or *ponder*, and combined with the negative prefix *"a"* means *not thinking, no thinking,* or *without thinking.*

   So we see that amusement literally means to not think, to not meditate, and to not think deeply. This is the total opposite of what we are supposed to do while we live our life and especially with the Scriptures. Now the *accuser* (i.e., Satan) knows that if we develop a habit of seriously meditating on God's Word, and we develop a habit of focusing on the Word and its meaning and application, we will become stronger. He is against that and will throw many amusements our way.

   As a side note, it is extremely interesting that today's worldly marketing strategy is not just to provide a good product, but to get people hooked on their *favorites,* so that they will spend an ever-increasing amount of time involved in enjoying and pursuing their favorite amusements. This is done in many ways. Just think how people get hooked on (also read – addicted to) their favorites: sports, web sites, TV shows, video games, foods, drinks, music groups, etc., not to mention the pursuit of material things and self-recognition. The list is seemingly endless.

While healthy diversions can be refreshing, we should make sure that *we* are in control of our amusement time and not vice versa.

We need to be careful to make sure that our amusements do not prevent us from spending quality time with the Lord and quantity time in ministering to others using our gifts and talents. In the case of some addictions, we may be literally fighting for our lives. If a journey of a thousand miles begins with one step, so it is with the gradual enslavement of our minds. It just does not happen overnight. And we cannot play the *victim card* here; because, we are not suddenly at the mercy of amusements, we have the choice each day.

We have stated before, "If God seems far away, guess who moved?" *If our time with God is not exciting, we may not be just living in the world, but we may be living like the world.* Pray that this will not happen.

Let's move on to *entertainment.*

The meanings of the two basic parts, *enter* and *tain,* are as follows: *enter* means *to be interlocked* or *connected*; and *tain* means *to hold.* Putting those together we get a picture of the mind being completely held and locked in place, not being able to do anything else but being fixated on that which entertains it.

The Biblical term lust actually shares the same idea in principle as entertainment. Lust is when we direct our minds to focus on one thing that we want. Entertainment is when we allow something to control our minds. Both activities trap the mind, and make it difficult for us to hear the voice of our Father God. Both represent are we make.

The Bible describes lusting as a battle, as a war against our very soul.

1 Peter 2:11 *Beloved, I urge you as aliens and strangers to abstain from fleshly lusts which wage war against the soul.*

Also as the following verses state, *we must be careful that the world does not dilute our most precious possession – the love of God.*

1 John 2:15,16 *Do not love the world nor the things in the world. If anyone loves the world, the love of the Father is not in him. For all that is in the world, the lust of the flesh and the lust of the eyes and the boastful pride of life, is not from the Father, but is from the world.*

Therefore we must understand that the battle is for our mind (also read heart, soul, mind, and strength). Thus, whether we are being amused (diverted from musing on the Lord's ways), or entertained, (our mind being held captive), both can prevent us from serving the Lord to our fullest capacity. The choice is ours. As we will see in the next section, how much fruit we bear for Christ is determined, in large part, by how *free* we truly are in Christ. We were not pardoned from sin so that we can indulge ourselves, but rather we were freed to serve others, as a true child of our Father.

Galatians 5:13 *For you were called to freedom,*
brethren; only do not turn your freedom into an
opportunity for the flesh, but through love serve
one another.

Our Fruit

Ever-increasing in God

As we follow His Word more closely, we enhance our friendship with the Lord. Our level of obedience to the Word does not make the Lord love us any more or any less. His love is unconditional. Our fellowship with Him, however, is much sweeter when we follow His Word and His Ways. If God seems far away — guess who moved? Seems we have heard that before!

Keep this in mind as we become familiar with His Word and His ways. Our goal is to develop a great lifelong eternal friendship with the Lord of Glory. We are not just learning rules and regulations, or facts and figures. We are getting to know the Person responsible for these words, and the one who created us, and thought we were so special that He would die for us, so that He could have the pleasure of our company!

To understand the diversity of responses to the Word of God throughout the world, let us look at the Parable of the Sower. Read Matthew 13:1-23, and then consider the following comparisons and commentary. These are nothing more than making some common-sense observations, and asking and answering some simple questions. This exercise will help us see the importance of Quiet Time and begin to teach us how to glean insights from the Word. Since the Gospels of Mark (chapter 4) and Luke (chapter 8) also carry this story, with slight but interesting differences, we have included a few insights from their versions as well.

This parable is applicable for both seekers and believers. For seekers, those who are searching for the truth about God, this parable illuminates how it is possible to appear to be a born-again Christian while never having truly repented of sinful ways and never having confessed Jesus as Lord and Savior. For believers, this parable contains amazing principles for starting and finishing the race well and for maximizing our fruitfulness.

A few times in this section, we will note that fruit is the ultimate outward sign of true belief.

That said, the ultimate reason we bear fruit is due to the indwelling Holy Spirit. We cannot see the wind, only the effect it has on things. Thus we cannot see the indwelling Spirit in others, only the effect He has on them. *A person controlled by the Holy Spirit will produce fruit. It will be unavoidable and unmistakable.*

  Our own fruitfulness is determined by many things. Read on!

Jesus speaks to the Crowds Matthew 13	Jesus speaks to the Disciples Matthew 13
1 That day Jesus went out of the house and was sitting by the sea. *2 And large crowds gathered to Him, so He got into a boat and sat down, and the whole crowd was standing on the beach.*	*18 Hear then the parable of the sower.*
3 And He spoke many things to them in parables, saying, "Behold, the sower went out to sow; *4 and as he sowed, some seeds fell beside the road, and the birds came and ate them up.*	*19 When anyone hears the word of the kingdom and does not understand it, the evil one comes and snatches away what has been sown in his heart. This is the one on whom seed was sown beside the road.*

Commentary:

Even if we were not privy to the interpretation given by Jesus to the disciples, we could glean some things from just meditating on what Jesus said to the crowds, and by asking questions. Why were the birds able to eat the seeds? Two obvious reasons are that they could see them; and they were able to pick them up without anyone or anything getting in their way. So we could come to the conclusion that if the seeds were completely buried in the soil the birds would not have been able to even see them, let alone snatch them up. Or, if the seeds were only partially buried, but still visible, perhaps if someone or something would be there to protect the seeds from the birds, then the seeds would also be safe from being snatched away.

The spiritual application of this would be obvious if we relate the Word to the seed and the heart to the soil. When the sower (God or one of His messengers) preaches the Word (the seed), we must make sure that our heart (the soil) is receptive to the Word, so that it goes deep into our heart. Even if we have doubts, which could be representative of the seed not completely buried, we must guard ourselves from those doubts (the birds); otherwise the Word (seed) will be removed from our heart (soil).

Jesus says essentially the same thing in principle. The evil one who will play on our doubts and our misunderstandings will try and get us to dismiss what was sown in our heart. If the Word is about salvation, and it is removed from our heart, we will miss an opportunity for salvation. If the Word is about spiritual growth, we will miss an opportunity to grow and bear fruit in a particular area.

Note that Mark (chapter 4) and Luke (chapter 8), which also carry this story, contain essentially the same thoughts. Luke adds that in addition to the birds eating the seeds, the seeds were trampled underfoot first. This trampling could be an illustration of how the Word may be corrupted or doubted even before it has a chance to get into the soil (heart).

In Jesus' discussion with His disciples, Luke adds that not only does the devil take away the Word from the heart of those who have heard it, but he does this so that they will not believe and be saved. This puts a specific evangelistic emphasis on the parable.

Jesus speaks to the Crowds Matthew 13	Jesus speaks to the Disciples Matthew 13
5 Others fell on the rocky places, where they did not have much soil; and immediately they sprang up, because they had no depth of soil.	*20 The one on whom seed was sown on the rocky places, this is the man who hears the word and immediately receives it with joy;*
6 But when the sun had risen, they were scorched; and because they had no root, they withered away.	*21 yet he has no firm root in himself, but is only temporary, and when affliction or persecution arises because of the word, immediately he falls away.*

Commentary:

Without hearing Jesus' special insights to His disciples, we can glean a few things by asking questions. Why do seeds falling on rocky places with little soil spring up so quickly? Well, if we think about it, most seeds when they germinate spend some time underground developing their root system before they pop out of the ground. So we do not see them immediately but only after a few days to a week or so. But for the seeds sown without much soil, the resulting plant will be visible right away. This is what it means that they immediately sprang up. Follow this up with another question: Why is it helpful to stay underground for awhile? Before the plant is subjected to the sun, wind and beating of the falling rain, it needs to make sure it is anchored to the soil securely and has a steady supply of water to make sure its stem and leaves have the strength to withstand whatever comes their way. The spiritual application to this is obvious. Growth is a long process and takes commitment. *The long haul cannot be fueled just by emotion, but by devotion.*

While Mark parallels Matthew, Luke again tends to summarize things, by saying only the *...seed fell on rocky soil, and as soon as it grew up, it withered away, because it had no moisture.* Notice it does not say anything about a root or the sun, but the picture is still clear.

Greek Speek:

temporary - the Greek word is πρόσκαιρος (*proskairos*). The word *temporary* in verse 21, in the Greek means *for a time,* or *for a season*; thus the root exists for only a specified time.

affliction - the Greek word is θλῖψις (*thlipsis*), other verses where this word is used (cross references) include Acts 7:10, 11:19, 14:22, Romans 8:35.

persecution - the Greek word is διωγμός (*diōgmos*), cross references include Mark 10:30, Acts 8:1, Romans 8:35.

falls away - the Greek word is σκανδαλίζω (*skandalizo*), note that the words *he falls away* literally mean *to be offended by.*

   This brings a slightly different connotation to the verse. Without knowing the Greek, you might think that the person is falling away because his new-found faith is too weak to hold up to the affliction and persecution. But in reality, the Greek suggests that the person is *unwilling* (not unable) to associate with being a Christian if it means that he will be afflicted or persecuted for his belief. He (immediately) does not like it one bit.

It is extremely interesting to read Paul's statement in Romans 8:35 in light of this.

Romans 8:35 *Who will separate us from the love of Christ? Will tribulation* (thlipsis*), or distress, or persecution* (diogmos), *or famine, or nakedness, or peril, or sword?*

Note that Paul says that tribulation and persecution (among other things) cannot separate us from the love of Christ; and yet, it is these very things that cause the person with no root to fall away. So what determines our response to persecution and affliction? That, my friend, is a question to ponder.

Final Thoughts:

While Mark again parallels Matthew in verse 21, Luke adds a thought, ...*and these have no firm root; they believe for a while, and in time of temptation fall away.*

The question to ask with Luke's narrative is: Is temporary belief, really belief at all? If you will follow the Word when it is convenient and not embarrassing, are you really a follower of the Word and a true disciple? It is interesting to note that Luke is basically equating the root with belief; in other words, no lasting root — no true belief.

Again this has applications for both seekers and believers. For seekers it explains why it may appear that they may have *found the faith* but really they do not possess a true saving faith. For believers, it is a warning to have our roots firmly established as in the teaching found in

Colossians 2:6,7 *Therefore as you have received Christ Jesus the Lord, so walk in Him having been firmly rooted and now being built up in Him and established in your faith, just as you were instructed, and overflowing with gratitude.*

Jesus speaks to the Crowds Matthew 13	Jesus speaks to the Disciples Matthew 13
7 Others fell among the thorns, and the thorns came up and choked them out.	*22 And the one on whom seed was sown among the thorns, this is the man who hears the word, and the worry of the world and the deceitfulness of wealth choke the word, and it becomes unfruitful.*

Commentary:

Note that Matthew 13:7 and the corollary in Luke state that the thorns choked the seed(s) *out*. Mark however, states that the thorns choked the seed and specifically mentions that it yielded no crop. This zero crop yield is implied in Matthew and Luke. Let us now look collectively at what Matthew, Mark and Luke say about what causes the Word to be choked out of our life.

Causes of choking

Matthew: worry of the world; deceitfulness of
wealth

Mark: worries of the world, deceitfulness of
riches, the desires for other things

Luke: worries and riches and pleasures of
this life

Taking all three Gospels together, the main
causes of choking are: Worry, wealth, riches,
desire for other things, and pleasures. A
question to ponder: What do entertainment,
amusement, worry, pursuit of wealth and
pleasure, and the desire for other things have
in common? Look at the following list and
ponder this.

Action	*Effect on the Mind*
Worry	strangle, constrict
Pursuit	blocks out
Amuse	prevent, restrict
Desire	captivate
Entertain	lock, trap

Greek Speek:

Choke

   There are three different words for choke used between the three gospels for this passage.

   πνίγω *(pnigō)*, the generic word for *choke*.

   ἀποπνίγω *(apopnigō)*, uses a more descriptive form of the verb using the preposition *apo* implying choking off, smothering, i.e., choking unto death.

   συμπνίγω *(sumpnigō)*, a more descriptive form of the verb employing the preposition *sun* (written as *sum* before the consonant *p*) implying choking together, or the idea that the thorns are ganging up on (crowding around) the plant.

   All three Gospels use *sumpnigō* for the word *choke* <u>when Jesus is talking to His disciples.</u> This probably signifies that worry, the pursuit of wealth, and pleasure will collectively *gang up* on us to choke out the Word. Interestingly

45

<u>when Jesus is talking to the crowds</u>, Matthew uses *pnigō* for *choke*, Luke uses *apopnigō*, and Mark uses *sumpnigō*.

Now let us look at a few more words from the passage: worry, wealth and unfruitful.

Worry

μέριμνα *(merimna)* is the Greek word and it is generally translated as *worry, care or anxiety*. It is interesting to note that our English word "worry" had its early origins as a verb meaning to strangle or constrict. This is exactly what the thorns are doing to us.

Wealth

πλοῦτος *(ploutos)* is the Greek word and refers to *wealth, riches, abundance, fullness*; with respect to the abundance of one's possessions, it would thus equate to one's personal wealth.

Unfruitful

ἄκαρπος *(akarpos)* is the Greek word that
Matthew and Mark use which is a negative
noun. The alpha *(a)*, at the beginning is the
negative meaning *no* or *without*. The Greek
word καρπος *(karpos)* means *fruit*. So the
meaning is *no fruit, without fruit,* or *fruitless.*

Luke uses *bring no fruit to maturity.* Luke
puts a slightly different meaning into this part
of the story. He indicates that the thorns gang
up and choke the seed/plant (the Word) so that
the fruit does not come to maturity or
completion. Now the purpose of a plant is to
bear fruit, so if the fruit never matures it is
essentially worthless. The point is clear: thorns
will spur the development of only immature
fruit or prevent fruit from growing altogether.
Perhaps Luke's description of immature fruit
could also be a good analogy of someone who
could appear as a Christian bearing fruit, but in
reality the fruit is not genuine, not useful, and
not produced by the Holy Spirit.

Final thoughts:

For seekers this means that despite an initial outward appearance of growth, there was no solid belief that could outlast the surrounding trappings. Isaiah says many times in his book that the people had eyes to see but did not see, and ears to hear but did not hear. It is no wonder, as their quest of worldly pleasures and the anxieties that are associated with that pursuit completely captivated their mind, making it impossible for the Holy Spirit to convict them of sin, righteousness and judgment (see John 16:8). For believers, we must be on guard, since we will be attacked on our weakest front. Thus we will not bear much fruit if we allow the things of the world to choke the Word. We may need to do some serious "weeding" in our lives.

Jesus speaks to the Crowds Matthew 13	Jesus speaks to the Disciples Matthew 13
8 And others fell on the good soil and yielded a crop, some a hundredfold, some sixty, and some thirty. 9 "He who has ears, let him hear."	*23 And the one on whom seed was sown on the good soil, this is the man who hears the word and understands it; who indeed bears fruit and brings forth, some a hundredfold, some sixty, and some thirty.*

Commentary:

Both Matthew 13:8 and its parallel in Mark 4 mention the increase as 30-, 60- and 100-fold; while Luke just mentions a 100-fold increase. Also in the explanation in Matthew 13:23 and in Mark 4, the 30-, 60-, and 100-fold increase is mentioned, while Luke does not even mention a specific increase, but states that the seed bore fruit *with perseverance.* It is interesting to note in the Gospels how the soil (hearts of people) received the seed (Word), as summarized below:

Matthew: Hear and Understand
Mark: Hear and Accept
Luke: Hear (in an honest and good heart)
          and Hold it Fast

All of the Gospels mention *hear*, but the next word describing how they received the Word is different among the Gospels. Matthew uses almost a neutral description of how they received it (i.e., *understand*), that by itself does not necessarily imply acceptance or belief. Mark states the acceptance, but does not indicate the level of commitment.

Luke 8:15 seems to make it crystal clear, *But the seed in the good soil, these are the ones who have heard the word in an honest and good heart, and hold it fast, and bear fruit with perseverance.*

While Luke does make it more clear how the Word was received, we already know how it was received, by the action that it produced. Thus even if the Scripture had only said, "this is the man who hears the Word and bears fruit," we would already know a lot by meditating on "bears fruit." We would know that the Word was sown deep into the heart of the individual. In all likelihood strong roots developed, and a continual supply of faith was turned into practice that yielded much fruit of the Spirit.

The ultimate outward sign of true belief has and always will be bearing fruit. This discussion on Quiet Time does not permit a lengthy discussion of fruit. However, please look at the following list (taken from Galatians 5:22, 23): *love, joy, peace, patience, kindness, goodness, faithfulness, gentleness, self-control.* Since the first fruit mentioned in the verse is love, and since Paul mentions in 1 Corinthians 13 that love is the *greatest*, we have also included in the Ezra 7¹⁰ Plan (Book 1) an in-depth study of love, to encourage our personal growth in this area.

Another aspect of fruit is that it contains seeds. These seeds can then be planted to grow even more fruit, for an ever-increasing abundance of fruit. When we get to the point where God is using us to spread the seeds of our fruit, and we see this fruit reproduced in others, then truly our harvest will be plentiful. We will see new plants grow (new believers), and existing plants flourish (growing disciples), all as a result of God blessing our fruitfulness.

The following tables sum up the passage that we have been studying. It is quite clear from this summary, as we have stated before, that fruit is the true outward indicator of saving faith, and of a true believer. For seekers, the Word that is being snatched, burnt or choked is the Word of salvation that is able to atone for their sin and make them born again as a true child of God.

But also for believers, this is a good picture of how some branches in our life seem to take forever to bear fruit. The key is the interest and the initial response. We may put some of the Word deep into our hearts, but other parts of Scripture we may struggle with applying.

Summary of the Parable of the Sower

Seed Sown	Interest	Initial Response	Final Response
Path (Hard Soil)	Hear Only	No desire to understand	Stays away
On Rocky Places	Hear Only	Emotional	Quickly falls away
In Thorns	Hear Only	Intellectual	Pursues other things
In Good Soil	Hear, Under-stand, Obey, Teach	Willful, Intellectual, Emotional	Follows the Word

Seed Sown	Final condition of seed or plant	Reasons
Path (Hard Soil)	Snatched away	Hard Hearted
On Rocky Places	Scorched	Offended by Trouble and Persecution
In Thorns	Choked	Worries, Pursuit of Wealth, Pleasure
In Good Soil	Growing, Fruit bearing	Faith, Obedience

Believers bear fruit and mature believers bear much fruit. As we may discern from the list of fruit in Galatians mentioned above, it does not mention money, business success, and personal skills as fruit. As believers, we must be aware that the fruit of the Spirit *is the list that counts!* All of the things that we have achieved in this world will pale in comparison to achieving (bearing) fruit. It is the fruit in our life, these character qualities that emulate the person of God, that will bless us, and more importantly, will make us a true blessing to others.

Jesus says that we can tell where a person stands by watching for the fruit. In the following passage Jesus talks about how we can discern between true and false prophets, but it is also applicable for discerning between true believers and false believers.

Matthew 7:16-20 *You will know them by their fruits. Grapes are not gathered from thorn bushes nor figs from thistles, are they? So every good tree bears good fruit, but the bad tree bears bad fruit. A good tree cannot produce bad fruit, nor can a bad tree produce good fruit. Every tree that does not*

bear good fruit is cut down and thrown into the
fire. So then, you will know them by their fruits.

Now in some cases we cannot always be sure, because we cannot see into a person's heart. We should never judge people based on a few actions, but over time. And we should never give up on people, period. That is for God Himself to decide.

The tables above will also give us some insight into how we will be attacked to prevent the seed from growing into maturity. The very Word that brings life to us may be snatched away because we have made no time to grab it. In some cases our initial excitement about following the Word in a particular area may be met with ridicule or pessimism, which will cause us to lose this fervor, and our root being scorched dies and our enthusiasm dies with it. In other cases, we solidly believe the Word in a certain area of our life, and begin to pursue it, but then we become busy with the things of this world. Slowly but surely, our convictions become buried and choked by other seemingly more important or pressing concerns, and our pursuit of the Word dies from suffocation. In some cases God Himself may be desperately trying to get through to us. But instead of making time to hear and understand what He is saying we allow other things to take away this time.

This in part may help to explain why there is variability in fruitfulness from one person to the next. Both our understanding and our obedience will determine our fruitfulness. We can be very obedient to the Word, but if we have read or studied very little of the Bible we will not produce as much fruit. Conversely, if we study and understand the Bible from cover to cover, and yet we pick and choose only what we want to obey, we will not bear as much fruit as possible.

We will explain this in mathematical terms. If complete understanding of the Bible on a scale of 1 to 10 equals a 10, and complete obedience on a scale of 1 to 10 equals a 10, then let us say fruitfulness is the *product* of understanding times obedience. Thus absolute understanding met with perfect obedience yields maximum fruitfulness (i.e., 10 x 10 = 100 QED). Using this example, and knowing that we are all not "perfect tens" in both categories, shows how we can have this variability in fruitfulness. All formulas aside, to produce fruit continuously, we simply must continue to increase our understanding of the Word of God, and continuously put it into action.

Now, this is obviously a bit simplistic; and yet, following Jesus is not really supposed to be complicated. One important additional way to become fruitful should be mentioned here. That is the way of faith.

There are times when we will not initially understand the Word or we will think that it may be impossible for us to obey a certain teaching. This is where faith comes in. We can obey the Word because the Word itself is trustworthy. It will never fail us. We can obey the Word because we know the Lord will only ask us to do something that He knows is possible, and is in our best interests. Each time we step out in faith, even when we do not understand or are fearful, the Lord will confirm that following His Word yields the best results.

In this way we build our confidence in the
Word, we build our faith in the Lord, and of
course, we will bear much fruit.

As we get to know Christ, our desire will grow
to be like Him in all ways, and will eventually
cause us to bear much fruit. It is hoped we will
heed the warnings in the *Parable of the Sower*
and make sure as we spend time with the Lord
and His Word, we seek to understand it fully,
accept it, hold it fast, and joyfully put it into
fruitful practice as His disciple and friend.

John 15:12-17 *This is My commandment, that you love one another, just as I have loved you. Greater love has no one than this, that one lay down his life for his friends. You are My friends if you do what I command you. No longer do I call you slaves, for the slave does not know what his master is doing; but I have called you friends, for all things that I have heard from My Father I have made known to you. You did not choose Me but I chose you, and appointed you that you would go and bear fruit, and that your fruit would remain, so that whatever you ask of the Father in My name He may give to you. This I command you, that you love one another.*

Our Focus

Every Day with God

So how do we spend time with God? We know how to spend time with our friends and family, yet to some of us, spending time with God seems so foreign and we find ourselves at a loss as to how this is done.

While there are many ways to do this, just as there are many ways to spend quality time with friends, perhaps it is best to focus on what we want to accomplish.

First, we want to know God. This is best accomplished by reading the Bible. But more than just reading, we want to focus on understanding the character and purposes of God. We should learn his commands for us, and the actions that He has taken on our behalf. But more importantly, we should try and understand *why* He commands us to do certain things, and *why* He acts in certain ways in certain circumstances. The Bible in some sense is like God's autobiography. The more we understand the why, the more we will really know the Lord; and we will begin to see His unmistakable fingerprints on our lives and the lives of others.

We will be able to discover what is true and false, what is prophecy and what is heresy, and what is sound doctrine and what is false doctrine. The best way to discern the genuine from the fake is to know the genuine so well that it is easy to spot any imitation.

It is comforting to know that the Bible says that God never changes. This is a true statement. God displays many moods in the Bible, but He is always consistent. For example, He does not display anger inappropriately, nor does He forgive indiscriminately.

Knowing how God deals with others will help us discern how He is dealing with us.

Second, we want to know what He wants us to do as His disciple and as a child of God. As we begin to see who He is, and what He wants us to do in general, we will begin to discern what He wants us to do in particular. For example, we know that He wants us to pray, but perhaps He may want us to pray for a particular person, church or ministry. We know He wants us to work to pay for living expenses, but perhaps there is a particular job He wants us to do. We know He wants us to minister to others, but perhaps there is a particular ministry He wants us involved with. Also, included in telling us in particular what He wants us to do, we simply must be able to discern when God is telling us to avoid something.

To accomplish this, as we read the Bible we should always be asking ourselves if God is trying to tell us something about our current circumstances. God not only wants us to know Him, He wants to instruct us daily on what lies ahead that day, and perhaps even prepare us for events in the future.

Keeping our Focus — Sharpening our Focus

Probably the biggest reason people do not *hear* the Holy Spirit, is that they do not spend time with God on a consistent basis, and they

do not spend time really meditating on what
the Word is saying to them in particular. God is
trying to speak to them through the Holy Spirit,
but it is as though they are hearing only every
third or fourth word, because they are not
spending enough time with God to be able to
discern anything.

One of the things we will discover as we
spend consistent time with God is that we will
see how God is dealing with us and our
circumstances in a way that is unique to us.
God does this for His children so that they can
clearly recognize that it is the Lord's
handiwork, and not just fate or luck or
something else. He will affirm and confirm our
prayers, answer our doubts, and ease our fears
in a way that we will know that it is
unmistakably from God. The Bible is very clear
on this. A heart that desires to understand God
will understand God. Eyes that desire to see
God, to see him act in their life and the lives of
others, will see God act. Ears that long to hear
that still small voice of God will hear, even
amidst the noise of the world. When we seek
him with all our heart we will find Him.

Although we touched on barriers to knowing
God such as amusement and entertainment,
there are other barriers that prevent us from
properly understanding what God is trying to
say to us. We ourselves can become a barrier to
a close relationship with God if we lose the
desire to bear fruit and lose our trust in Him. It
all starts when we begin to go our own way. We
must remember that although our Father
wants to bless us materially, He is more
interested that we bear spiritual fruit, and that
we follow His ways.

Instead of spending consistent time with God
discerning His will we may justify our actions
and lack of fruit by saying things such as: *I am
not as bad as this other person* (justifying our
bad habit because it is not as bad as another's);
or *this other person is making me this* way
(meaning I don't have to take responsibility for
my actions); or *I just cannot do what God is
asking me to do* (meaning I do not trust or
believe that God will help me grow in this
area).

Another way that we subtly go astray is that
we just do whatever we think is best and let

God sort it out. We can start to think that God helps those who help themselves, which is not in the Bible, and reflects the thinking of someone who still wants to be in charge of his or her life. The Old Testament especially is full of examples of people who say they want to follow God's ways, but in reality they want what they desire or what makes them feel comfortable. These people try to justify their actions by using nice-sounding excuses, or by following what they think their image of God would say or do in a particular situation.

So how do we misinterpret what God is trying to say to us? Well, for example, God may be trying to get us to break a bad habit, but we do not see it that way, or we do not think we can do it. So instead of following a tougher course of action we may take the easy way out or do nothing.

A multitude of examples of this are in the Old Testament. His usual way of reminding us of needed changes in our life is through the Word, our daily Quiet Time, church, music, other believers, and sometimes circumstances. He does not delight in tripping people up to teach them, but He may use any method if He sees that we are starting to get complacent, and our mind, eyes and ears are starting to close.

One of the reasons David was a man after God's own heart was not that he was perfect. When David was challenged on a particular bad action or behavior, he did not make excuses, but fully agreed with God that he was in the wrong and willingly accepted his discipline. Fully agreeing with God about what is wrong, and turning away from our sinful actions, is the true definition of repentance. Just saying we are sorry does not necessarily mean we agree that what we did was wrong. Now God is not just trying to ping us for every little step we take off the straight and narrow. He gives us leeway to stray a little and then He will gently bring us back. It is hoped we will recognize this because we are in touch with Him on a daily basis with an open heart. Only when we seem to be developing a pattern of going our own way does He step up the discipline, just as a good father should.

To further this discussion let us look at the example of the Nation of Israel after they had been set free from their bondage in Egypt. That is symbolic of our being set free from the bondage of sin. Although God did promise them that they would be traveling to the Promised Land where they would experience material blessing, it was always predicated on following His ways as stated in the Law, the Books of Moses. The wilderness journey was a chance for each person to get to know God and His ways, and to develop a close relationship with his Lord. If we closely follow the journey, we will see that God was a very visible presence day and night. He desired a close relationship with His true children. His main goal was to teach them what it meant to be a child of God. But a great majority of the people cared only about the blessing part. They did not want to experience thirst or hunger or fear. They wanted all these things eliminated.

While God was trying to train up these children, the majority of the people wanted nothing of it. They completely missed what God was trying to accomplish for good in their lives. We should remember this before we start

getting into a pattern where we are constantly
asking God to bless us and answer our prayers
so that we can do what *we* want instead of what
our *Father* wants.

James 4:3 *You ask and do not receive, because you
ask with wrong motives, so that you may spend it
on your pleasures.*

 Very subtly over time, we can begin to think
that God is *our* resource who will give us what
we want so that we can live how *we* want. God
does desire to bless us, but He is more
concerned that we bear spiritual fruit.

 Before we start off on the wrong foot, it is best
to realize that God wants us to bear fruit, such
as love, joy, peace, patience, kindness,
goodness, faithfulness, gentleness, and self-
control. And for many of us who need work in
these areas, one way to develop character is to
experience adversity, in order to foster
character growth. Thus, the next time we face
the same adversity, we can more easily face it
because of our more mature behavior and
outlook. The following scenarios will give us
some further insight into how God encourages

and admonishes us to grow in His character, as we grow in our relationship with Him.

Let us start with the person who is just starting off on a new life in Christ. To encourage us to grow in a particular area the Lord will teach us through His Word, and other people, and as we take baby steps in the right direction He will most likely bless each correct step we take. He will continue this blessing as our actions turn into good habits. He may also bring people into our lives that exhibit very mature fruit that we admire so as to spur us on to be like Christ. That is just like the Lord to bring mentors our way to show us good visible examples. Daily Quiet Time helps us to recognize that this is what the Lord is doing for us!

Now what happens when we start developing bad character habits? Perhaps instead of being encouraged by other people, we try to find faults in them in order to justify why we do not listen to them. By overlooking even their good qualities we are missing God's messages to us through them. God may then try to show us where we are lacking in character by sending people into our lives that exhibit the same poor character qualities that we have. To those of us who are constantly angry, He may send angry people. For those of us who constantly criticize people, He may send people our way that do not encourage us in our good deeds, but will only criticize our failings. We may see the light and change our behavior. But conversely, instead of seeing ourselves in their actions, we may just criticize their poor behavior, not knowing that we act the same way. God will be creative and will never stop until we recognize our bad behavior and truly repent. This process may take awhile. That time frame though is up to us.

And finally, what about those mature believers who are progressing well? Does God just leave them alone? He will bless their efforts of course, but God will continue to strengthen even their strengths. One key way is through adversity. God may place adversity or poor character examples in front of us to show us our bad sides, but He may also place adversity in our path (even if we are walking well) to make sure that we are still growing deeper in His character. He is exhorting us to be holy, simply because He is holy. One of the signs of a mature believer is that we do things for the Lord, less and less for the blessings that follow, but more and more just to please our Father. The Lord will allow us to experience circumstances that challenge our motives. If we follow God only when blessings follow, then our growth will eventually suffer. The Lord gently guides us into a more committed relationship and to a point where we are capable of withstanding just about anything, while still bearing much fruit. Again, daily Quiet Time is the only way we will continue to progress into an ever-deepening relationship with the Lord. And what a full and exciting life it will be! For example, while the lives of Moses, David and Paul ran the gamut of experiences, they would all agree that living for the Lord is the most fulfilling thing we can ever do.

We need to ask ourselves how often we beg God to give us more love, or more patience, or more kindness. This is what we need to focus on. Brother Lawrence (Nicholas Herman) reminds us of this in a book (*The Practice of the Presence of God: The Best Rule of Holy*

Life) containing several of his conversations
and letters. Some excerpts follow:

*That many do not advance in the Christian
progress because they stick in penances, and
particular exercises, while they neglect the
love of God, which is the end...That there
needed neither art nor science for going to
God, but only a heart resolutely determined to
apply itself to nothing but Him, or for His
sake, and to love Him only. — from the Third
Conversation*

*That we ought not to be weary of doing little
things for the love of God, who regards not the
greatness of the work, but the love with which
it is performed. — from the Fourth
Conversation*

*That the greater perfection a soul aspires
after, the more dependent it is upon Divine
Grace. — from the Fourth Conversation*

*God knoweth best what is needful for us, and
all that He does is for our good. If we knew
how much He loves us, we should be always*

ready to receive equally and with indifference from His hand the sweet and the bitter, all would please that came from Him. The sorest afflictions never appear intolerable, but when we see them in the wrong light. When we see them in the hand of God, who dispenses them when we know that it is our Father who abases and distresses us; our sufferings will lose their bitterness, and become even [a] matter of consolation.

Let all our employment be to know God; the more one knows Him, the more one desires to know Him. And as knowledge is commonly the measure of love, the deeper and more extensive our knowledge shall be, the greater will be our love; and if our love of God were great we should love Him equally in pains and pleasures.

Let us not amuse ourselves to seek or to love God for any sensible favours (how elevated soever) which He has or may do us. Such favours, though never so great, cannot bring us so near to God as faith does in one simple act. Let us seek Him often by faith. He is within us; seek Him not elsewhere. Are we not

*rude and deserve blame, if we leave Him
alone, to busy ourselves about trifles, which do
not please Him and perhaps offend Him? "Tis
to be feared these trifles will one day cost us
dear.*

*Let us begin to be devoted to Him in good
earnest. Let us cast everything besides out of
our hearts; He would possess them alone. Beg
this favour of Him. If we do what we can on
our parts, we shall soon see that change
wrought in us which we aspire after. — from
the Fifteenth Letter, two days before his death
at age 86 in the year 1691 AD.*

To echo what Brother Lawrence says about
God doing things for our good, consider
someone who may be praying for a certain type
of job, or looking for prestige or for a certain
situation to change that God knows would
actually be bad for him. The Lord will frustrate
his plans until he realizes that the goal is not
getting what he wants, but pressing on towards
what he needs to be.

If our self-made plans will affect our growth
as a believer negatively, then as a good father

He will make sure those plans do not succeed. Sadly many of us are so wrapped up in our own plans that we have to experience failure after failure until we realize that we are acting like the Israelites in the desert. God does not want us to fail, but if failure is the only way He can get our attention, then He will allow us to fail. Our spiritual growth is the most important thing to God. He does not mind pruning some bad branches in order for us to experience optimum growth. We can avoid this constant pruning if we yield to His ways early on. We should not stubbornly insist on our own way or say we just cannot follow God's ways, because they are too hard for us or we are too afraid to trust Him. As Brother Lawrence says, *Let us begin to be devoted to Him in good earnest.*

Two great verses to pray every day are what David penned in Psalm 139:

Psalm 139:23, 24 *Search me, O God, and know my heart; Try me and know my anxious thoughts; And see if there be any hurtful way in me, And lead me in the everlasting way.*

In summary: We want to know God, we want to know what He wants us to do as His disciple, and as we keep and sharpen our focus we want to reflect His character in what we do as a faithful child of our Father. Quiet Time helps us accomplish this.

Build Consistency with Goals and Structure

We can start off well if we set some solid goals. For example, we can plan for one week or one month that we will not miss our Quiet Time no matter what. Once we complete a week or month, we will be amazed at the difference, and it is hoped we will begin a lifelong habit that will transform our life forever as we see God as never before.

Ephesians 2:10 *For we are God's workmanship, created in Christ Jesus to do good works, which God prepared in advance for us to do.*

So now that we have set the time aside, what are some good practical things to do during our time with God?

Here are a few ideas:

- ➤ Spend a minimum of 15 minutes and watch it grow to 30 minutes or longer
- ➤ Pick or make a time of the day that we know is most often free from distractions
- ➤ Use a Bible-reading plan (We may want to start in the New Testament, but we should try and read through the entire Bible every year)
- ➤ Write notes in our Bible as we read
- ➤ Keep a Quiet Time journal of thoughts
- ➤ Spend a few minutes after we read, meditating and praying about what we just read, reflecting on how it applies to us and to our particular circumstances

And throughout the day we may:

- ➤ Memorize a Scripture that we read that day
- ➤ Pray for others
- ➤ Be watchful for God to answer our prayers
- ➤ Tell another person about our time with God

Final thoughts on keeping our focus...

We need to resist the impulse of turning our Quiet Time into just something that is on our to-do list. Our time with God needs to be unhurried. As we read through selected portions of the Bible, we need to have the time to meditate on the Word, ask God questions, reflect on what it means, etc. We should not feel that we have to hurry up and read a few chapters of the Bible. Perhaps during our Quiet Time God will ask us to pray for certain people or to look up some Bible cross references. We may even feel moved to sing or play a song. We need to have the freedom (from tight time constraints) to go where God may be leading us. And let us not think that we need to limit ourselves to just one Quiet Time a day.

Why did we recommend (not require) 15 minutes? Well, for several reasons. Sadly, today we actually have well-meaning Christian authors who develop devotions for people on the go that only take five or six minutes of our time. We have other publications advertising quick and easy ways to get our devotion time in. This is sad really. Firstly, it is turning a special time into some type of Pharisaical regulation. Secondly, it implies that the process of spiritual growth can somehow be shortened. Lastly, it is an insult to the Lord of Glory that we would want to spend so little time with Him after all He has done for us. Remember, God has gone to great lengths for us, and we should be willing to go to great lengths for Him.

No, my friends, 15 minutes is by no means a lot of time. We can just ask ourselves that if getting to know God is priority one in our life, would 5 minutes a day really reflect that priority? For example, if exercising to get in shape was a priority, would spending 5 minutes a day exercising reflect that priority? I think we know the answer.

Put another way, if God called us or sent us an e-mail and said He would really like to meet with us every day for an hour, would we be there? Would we make the time? Oh I think we would! Let us start with 15 minutes and see how it grows from there.

Your Father is really looking forward to it!

Our Field

Explaining God

Keep it Simple

This book has taught us much about Quiet Time, the benefits, the pitfalls to avoid, and how to put it into practice. But if we take an additional step and prepare a small teaching in order to instruct others we will help solidify this activity in our lives and in the lives of others. Preparing ourselves to teach others what we have learned is a great way to accomplish Christ's *Great Commission* found in Matthew 28:19, 20.

Go therefore and make disciples of all the nations, baptizing them in the name of the Father and the Son and the Holy Spirit, teaching them to observe all that I commanded you; and lo, I am with you always, even to the end of the age.

In order to explain anything first we must decide on the major points of emphasis. We should also pick our time frame. We should develop one-minute and perhaps three-minute versions to be prepared for those casual conversations. We need to be able to hit the high points without going into too much detail.

   This book has been organized using easy-to-remember titles and sub-titles. Each title has two words, the first beginning with the letter "O" and the next with the letter "F." The sub-titles are equally easy to remember as the first word begins with the letter "E" and the last word begins with the letter "G."
   Strung together the titles and sub-titles are as follows:

Our Father:	Experiencing God
Our Failures:	Extinguishing God
Our Fruit:	Ever-increasing in God
Our Focus:	Every Day with God
Our Field:	Explaining God

   A possible outline of key points per section is included at the end of this discussion. We encourage everyone to develop individual outlines and key points as well. One easy way to pass on a particular teaching in just a few seconds is to memorize a few key points in each section. If the person we are talking to has more time or interest we can expand as he asks questions. By using easy-to-memorize titles and sub-titles it makes it that much easier to recall the material.

By being familiar with all the key points of each section we can tailor our conversation about Quiet Time depending on the needs of the individual. We may have to deal with different issues related to Quiet Time. For example, someone may need to know how to start; another person may not be getting a lot out of his Quiet Time and may need some encouragement. Someone who is completely unfamiliar with Quiet Time may ask us to explain the whole concept. We may see others who are allowing the ways of the world to crowd out their time with God and we can warn them of the pitfalls they are heading into and remind them of the blessings of Quiet Time. Of course if we are developing a more formal teaching on the subject of Quiet Time we can use the full outline and go into each key point more systematically and in more detail.

So our assignment is to use the outline at the end of this section as a guide, but to develop our own outline in our own words. It is fine to use some of the outline if needed. It is best to make the outline with its key points *our own* so we can more readily share it in our own unique way.

Motivate - Encourage

We should make it one of our goals to share some aspect of Quiet Time with another person each and every week! People are motivated to spend time with God when they see and hear of others doing the same thing. We should share the highs and lows (keep it real) as the apostle Paul says:

Philippians 4:11-13 *Not that I speak from want, for I have learned to be content in whatever circumstances I am. I know how to get along with humble means, and I also know how to live in prosperity; in any and every circumstance I have learned the secret of being filled and going hungry, both of having abundance and suffering need. I can do all things through Him who strengthens me.*

Our part in equipping new disciples will have eternal results! The harvest is indeed plentiful but the laborers are so few.

Perhaps we should think as Brother Lawrence has said that our real employment is to know God (and make Him known). Many people view serving the Lord as something they do only if there is time left after they go to work, fulfill other obligations, spend time with friends and family, etc.

How would it be if we told others that we are employed by God? Now what would happen if this was our true mind set? What if all of our earthly work that we do for pay, all our possessions, all of our friends and family, all our free time, were simply part of and subservient to our heavenly employment? Think about it.

The outline follows.

Quiet Time Outline

Our Father: Experiencing God
Why Our Father is worth our time
- *He never gives up on people*
- *He cares about us*
- *The Lord cherishes communing with us*
- *God has gone to great lengths for us, we should go to great lengths with Him*
- *It is exciting to see how He leads us*
- *He is our source of total supply*

Our Failures: Extinguishing God
Distractions from spending time with God
- *Amusement*
- *Entertainment*

Our Fruit: Ever-increasing in God

Insights from the Parable of the Sower

- *A person controlled by the Holy Spirit will produce fruit*
- *We must make sure that our heart is receptive to the Word, so that it goes deep into our hear – Hard Soil*
- *The long haul cannot be fueled just by emotion, but by devotion – Rocky Soil*
- *We will not bear fruit if we allow the things of the world to choke us – Thorny Soil*
- *Keys to fruit bearing: Hear the Word, Hold the Word in an Honest Heart – Good Soil*

Our Focus: Every Day with God

How to

- *Pick an unhurried time slot*
- *Spend a minimum of 15 minutes and watch it grow*
- *Pick or make a time of the day that we know is most often free from distractions*
- *Use a Bible-reading plan*
- *Write notes in our Bible as we read*
- *Keep a Quiet Time journal of thoughts*
- *Spend a few minutes after we read, meditating and praying about what we just read, reflecting on how it applies to us and to our particular circumstances*
- *Memorize a Scripture that we read that day*
- *Pray for others*
- *Be watchful for God to answer our prayers*
- *Tell another person about our time with God*

Bibliography

Aland, B., Aland, K., Black, M., Martini, C. M., Metzger, B. M., & Wikgren, A. (1993, c1979). *The Greek New Testament* (4th ed.). Federal Republic of Germany: United Bible Societies.

Herman, Nicholas (c. 1605-1691). The Practice of the Presence of God: The Best Rule of Holy Life. Public Domain.

Merriam-Webster, I. (1996, c1993). *Merriam-Webster's collegiate dictionary*. (10th ed.). Springfield, Mass., U.S.A.: Merriam-Webster.}

New American Standard Bible : 1995 update. 1995. LaHabra, CA: The Lockman Foundation.

Strong, J. (1996). *The exhaustive concordance of the Bible : Showing every word of the test of the common English version of the canonical books, and every occurence of each word in regular order.* (electronic ed.). Ontario: Woodside Bible Fellowship.

Swanson, J. (1997). Dictionary of Biblical Languages with Semantic Domains : Greek (New Testament) (electronic ed.). Oak Harbor: Logos Research Systems, Inc.

www.ingramcontent.com/pod-product-compliance
Lightning Source LLC
Chambersburg PA
CBHW070548030426
42337CB00016B/2410